Castle Coole

Co. Fermanagh

THE NATIONAL TRUST

Growing up at Castle Coole

by the Earl of Belmore

I had the very good fortune to grow up at Castle Coole, and my memory of the place slowly develops from the mid-1950s onwards. The National Trust's caretaker originally lived in part of the basement, and forays were often made down to Mr and Mrs Wright's kitchen around teatime, where large portions of fruit cake were liberally handed out. On the ground floor, my parents' staff lived in the east wing, as I did, as our nursery was situated there, and my parents and sisters slept elsewhere, with the result on any night there would be eleven people sleeping in the house right through to the late 1950s.

Tourism had not reached Fermanagh in the way it had reached Kerry, and few people actually came to marvel at Wyatt's masterpiece, so Mr Wright had time to read, mostly his own books on the Wild West, in the Library in front of an electric fire. Ex-King Leopold of the Belgians came to stay when I was about five years old, and this was a very exciting event. The King very kindly asked me what I would like, and being unprepared for this gesture,

The 7th Earl of Belmore (far left) at the Enniskillen Mart with his champion bullock in 1959

(Above) Ex-King Leopold of the Belgians planting a tree at Castle Coole

I suggested a sandpit would be well received. The pit was duly built by Sweeney, the estate carpenter, and I was presented with a bottle of orange squash as a bonus just before Leopold left. Those were the days…. However, this idyllic existence came to a dramatic halt in 1960, when our father suddenly died, and I was sent to boarding school in England.

But it was to Castle Coole I always endeavoured to return, as the 'pull' was so strong and memories so vivid, and we still had the good fortune of seeing our elderly cousins, who lived close by at Bellevue, but who had also grown up at Castle Coole in the Victorian era, along with their nine other brothers and sisters. Their afternoon teas were eagerly looked forward to, with homemade scones, cakes, followed by games such as 'Hunt the Thimble' and 'Old Maid'. I even remember a game of football with all four cousins acting as joint goalie, as I searched for a crack in their defence.

The cousins, Dorothy, Violet, Margaret and Winifred, were a great source of friendship to us all. The last of the four, Margaret, died in 1975, and we miss them dreadfully, for they were a direct link with the past: Queen Victoria, the Great War, not to mention the early Troubles in Ireland. Castle Coole was my family's only home, and this meant different generations never left for long.

My father handed the house to the National Trust in July 1951, and I can safely say the property has been maintained by the Trust to a very high standard ever since, with a dedicated staff, and the fabric of the building receiving much attention and expense in the 1980s. Over 70 percent of the Portland stone was renewed with limestone from the same quarries as the original; the house was rewired; and so now the visitor sees the result of the Wyatt/Belmore partnership at its best. Our eldest son John, born in 1985, has moved back into Castle Coole from the Garden House, so the family link continues.

The greatest Neo-classical country house in Ireland

A temple to good taste

As soon as you catch sight of Castle Coole's façade of crisp Portland stone rising from the hillside above Lough Coole, you are conscious that you are in the presence of something special. This is indeed a house for the connoisseur and a monument to the austere good taste of its creator.

Such perfection had its price. Built in 1789–97, it was meant to confirm the rise to wealth and power of Armar Lowry-Corry, 1st Earl of Belmore, whose great-great-grandfather had bought the manor of Coole in 1655. The 1st Earl had inherited three family estates, which comprised over 70,000 acres and generated an annual income of £11,000. But despite his great wealth, the 1st Earl was badly hit by the expense of building his dream house, and three years after it was completed, his national political influence evaporated with the abolition of the Irish parliament in Dublin.

(Right) The Saloon

Home and abroad

Although Castle Coole lies in the far north-west of the island of Ireland, it is an outward-looking building of world class. Its Neo-classical style of architecture is indebted to Greece, Rome and France. It is the masterpiece of an English architect, James Wyatt. The stone that clads the building came from Dorset. Even the craftsmen employed on decorating its interiors were mostly from far afield: the English plasterer Joseph Rose, the Italian scagliola-worker Domenico Bartoli and the English sculptor Richard Westmacott. Supervising the whole project was a Scotsman, Alexander Stewart.

When the 2nd Earl decided to refurnish the house in 1807, he chose a Dublin upholsterer, John Preston, and local craftsmen did most of the joinery. However, the pieces he commissioned at vast expense – gilt couches, chairs, tables, mirrors and torchères – were in a lavish French Empire style, and many of them were imported from London.

The Belmores also loved to travel – none more so than the 2nd and 4th Earls, who brought back souvenirs of their stays in Egypt and Syria, Jamaica and Australia, some of which are still to be seen at Castle Coole. And yet the tug of their ancestral home remained strong. They always returned to Castle Coole, and although the house was given to the National Trust in 1951, the present Lord Belmore and his family still live on the demesne and in part of the house and take an active interest in its future.

(Above) The entrance front

(Below, left) Armar, 1st Earl of Belmore (1740–1802), the builder of the house

(Below, right) Somerset, 2nd Earl of Belmore (1774–1841), who commissioned the magnificent Regency furniture

The Exterior

The entrance front

The entrance front faces up the hill away from the lough and comes into view only at the last moments of your arrival. The central block is nine bays wide and two storeys high. Unlike classical country houses of the previous generation, the basement is completely hidden from view so that the house appears to rise directly from the ground. The massive sloping roof of Welsh slate plays an unusually prominent part in the composition: it is uninterrupted by attic windows, which are hidden away behind the roof-top balustrade. Wyatt's designs even dispensed with chimneystacks, but these proved impossible to omit. The windows are particularly severe – plain rectangular openings with no moulding of any kind. Dominating the entrance front is the four-columned two-storey Ionic portico, with an unusual form of capital that is set at 45 degrees to the façade. The pediment above is completely plain.

Flanking the central block are straight, single-storey, colonnaded wings of the baseless fluted Doric Order, which end in pavilions that continue the Doric colonnade and are topped by balustrades answering that in the centre. The back walls of the colonnades are punctuated by semicircular niches, which have always been empty.

Crisply cut blocks of Portland stone were used to face the building throughout.

The park front

This looks north over the lough and first comes into view from below as you approach along the entrance drive. Instead of a portico, there is a central two-storey bow with fluted Ionic columns – a favourite Wyatt motif. The ground-floor sash-windows in the bow extend right down the floor to allow direct access from the Saloon to the park. The wings are just plain walls articulated by windows that are aligned with those on the ground floor of the central block. The side-pavilions have pretty Venetian windows with medallions above and further empty niches on either side.

(Above) The entrance front
(Right) The park front from across Lough Coole

The Interior

The Entrance Hall

This room immediately sets the tone of Neo-classical perfection, which is achieved not by ornament, but by symmetry, carefully judged proportions and the finest materials and craftsmanship. It is intended to resemble a Roman atrium, with a screen of smooth columns made from porphyry-coloured scagliola (imitation marble), which was supplied by Domenico Bartoli. Doric, the plainest of the classical orders, was chosen as most appropriate for an entrance hall. The niches were designed to display sculpture, but the 1st Earl preferred to leave them empty.

The room looked very different in the early 20th century, when it was furnished in the Victorian style, including cases of stuffed birds.

Decoration

Wyatt specified a bare Portland stone floor, a plain ceiling (painted the same colour as the floor), no curtains and only one fireplace. The result was a chilly, echoing space, and in the event a second fireplace was added in the east wall. The Carrara marble *fireplaces* were carved in London by Richard Westmacott at a cost of about £200 and shipped over in 1795. The chimneypiece and ceiling *friezes* are carved to match, with garlanded rosettes (from the old Corry coat of arms) and chalices (from the Lowry arms). Edward Stanley of Birmingham supplied the very fine brass *door furniture* on the mahogany doors.

Wyatt seems to have painted the *walls* a stony off-white colour. The present shade of porphyry was chosen to match the columns and is based on scrapes taken of a paint put on by Preston before 1816.

Preston supplied scarlet *curtains*, which remained in use until at least 1949.

'The furniture of a hall should... be bold, massive, and simple, yet noble in appearance, and introductory to the rest.'

Thomas Sheraton, *The Cabinet Dictionary*, 1803

The Entrance Hall

Lighting

The four white-painted *tripods* were meant to support candlesticks (there was never a ceiling light in this room). The original glass shades were rediscovered in the attic and returned. The tripods (or *athéniennes*) were designed by Wyatt and made in 1797–8 in the form of classical altar stands.

Furniture

The mahogany *hall-chairs* bear the Belmore coat of arms. (The griffin crest was adopted by the 1st Earl, but later abandoned.) They were probably designed by Wyatt and supplied by Kidd of Dublin. With their elegant 'sabre' legs, they are among the finest examples of Irish Neo-classical furniture. Hall-chairs had to be hard-wearing and were usually much more basic.

(Left) A Wyatt tripod

The hall-chairs were designed by Wyatt

The Morning Breakfast Room

This room started out as the family's private dining room, although it is hardly any smaller than the Dining Room. By 1872 it had been converted into a billiard room, but by the early 20th century the billiard-table was usually buried under piles of books. The ladies of the house also used this room for doing the flowers. It returned to its original function after 1949.

Decoration

Wyatt designed the ceiling plasterwork and the frieze of fluted reeds, which matches that over the doors. The plasterwork and woodwork were originally painted off-white. Preston painted the walls blue in Regency style. They have been repainted shades of blue at least twice since then.

Preston also supplied the curtain pole, which stretches the length of the window wall, and the chintz curtains printed with Chinoiserie scenes in yellow, green and red (a large swatch of which is displayed in the case to the right of the fireplace). The curtains had been removed by 1952, but the National Trust hopes to replace them.

In 1903 the skin of an Australian duckbill platypus was spread on the floor (the 4th Earl had been Governor-General of New South Wales).

Chimneypiece

This was again supplied by Westmacott, but is very different from Wyatt's design.

Furniture and ceramics

Wyatt seems to have designed no furniture specifically for the room.

The two black lacquer *bookcases* with their pagoda tops are a bizarre mixture of French, Chinese and Classical styles which is typically Regency. They were supplied by Preston and were probably always intended for their present position between the windows. They are now used to display oval *Derby dishes* and half of a *Chelsea dessert service*, both of *c*.1760. The other half of the Chelsea service is at nearby Florence Court, having been given to the 1st Earl's sister Anna on her marriage to the 1st Earl of Enniskillen in 1763.

The *sofa* is the 'large Grecian Couch with full suit of seat and back Cushions, Bolsters and feather Pillows' supplied by Preston for £45 10s. It was upholstered with Chinese chintz covers which survived until at least 1951. It was re-covered in the present blue fabric in 1980.

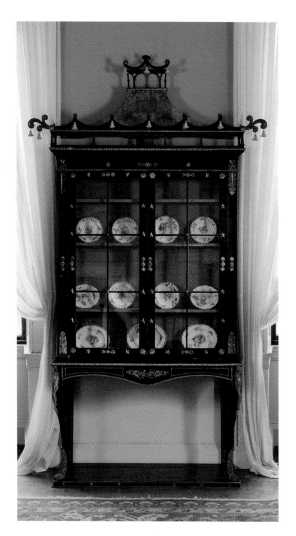

(Left) A Chinoiserie black lacquer bookcase in the Morning Breakfast Room

(Above) The Morning Breakfast Room

Pictures

Right of the door from the Entrance Hall is a full-length portrait of the **2nd Earl of Belmore**, painted by Hugh Douglas Hamilton in 1802. The large folio on the table behind him is the Act of Union between England and Ireland, which he strenuously opposed. Under his left hand is his address to the King on the subject. When the bill was finally passed in 1800, he declared, 'I hope I shall be permitted to avert my eyes in the last moment of the constitutional independence of my country.'

The Flight into Egypt over the fireplace is north Italian. The large painting on the far wall is *Castor and Pollux* by G.B. Cipriani. It depicts the 'heavenly twins', who were immortalised as the constellation Gemini. The picture was made for Houghton Hall in Norfolk. It was bought in 1990 by the present Lord Belmore and is a highly appropriate addition to the house, as Cipriani was a key proponent of the Neo-classical style in decorative painting.

The Dining Room

In the early 19th century, dinner was usually served at 5. According to a guest, it was 'very handsome and served on plate [i.e. silver]'. Menus included locally caught oysters, lobster and fish. Ice-cream was made with ice from the ice-house on the estate.

Decoration

This room is a very fine example of Wyatt's restrained Neo-classical style. The ceiling plaster-work (by Joseph Rose), frieze and dado subtly relate, using a common decorative language of husks, rosettes, guilloche (interlacing) bands and *tazzae* (shallow dishes). The walls are divided into simple rectangular panels. Wyatt painted them pale green. Preston repainted them grey. They are now green once again.

The *chimneypiece* was carved by Westmacott and shipped to Ireland in 1795 at a cost (including transport) of £130.

Wyatt did not intend there to be curtains, which were thought to retain the smell of stale food. However, the 2nd Earl commissioned curtains of 'best Scarlet Superfine Broad Cloth' with scarlet and black trimmings. These had gone by 1949 and have not been replaced.

The *carpet* was acquired by the National Trust in 1988.

Furniture and ceramics

The *sideboard* was designed by Wyatt to display the family silver, and made in 1797 by Henry McBrien and Barney McGirr. It is flanked by pedestals supporting urns, which were made by McGirr and John Moore and probably also designed by Wyatt. They are decorated with oval panels, possibly by Biagio Rebecca. By the 1790s, this arrangement, which followed that in Robert Adam's Eating Room of 1767 at Osterley Park in Middlesex, was decidedly old-fashioned.

(Right) The sideboard with wine-cooler below and urn on pedestal

The huge mahogany *wine-cooler* under the sideboard was also made in 1797 by Stewart, possibly to Wyatt's design. In the 18th century, red and white wine were both drunk chilled. The fluted decoration echoed that on Roman sarcophagi and was also much used on Neo-classical silver.

Wyatt's original dining-chairs were given away by the 2nd Earl, who wanted something more impressive. The present mahogany *table* with its ormolu lion's-paw feet was supplied by Preston for 200 guineas and is a superb piece of Regency design. The 2nd Earl commissioned silver of the highest quality to decorate his table, most famously a silver-gilt plateau with three tripod dessert stands, which was made in 1810 by Paul Storr to a design by Thomas Hope (now in the Al-Tajir collection). Today, the table displays a Copeland service. The tables flanking the fireplace show an 18th-century *Derby dessert service*.

The Regency *dining-chairs* were bought from Townley Hall, Co. Louth.

Pictures

Paintings were not hung here before 1951. There are now displayed portraits of 18th-century members of the Corry family: the 1st Earl's grandfather, *Col. John Corry*, and four of the latter's children, including *Sarah Corry*, whose marriage to Galbraith Lowry in 1733 united the Lowry and Corry families.

The Dining Room

The Saloon

This grand oval room is the focus of the house and the climax of the state apartments. It was used for important family occasions such as balls and receptions. The whole household – family and servants – held prayers here every morning before breakfast.

Curving rooms and bow windows are a defining characteristic of Wyatt's style, which he adapted from Robert Adam. A similar arrangement of centrally placed Entrance Hall and curved Saloon can be found at Adam's Kedleston Hall in Derbyshire, where Wyatt's elder brother Samuel had been the master-carpenter. Wyatt had made his own reputation with his circular Pantheon in London.

Decoration

As befits its status, this is the most elaborately decorated room in the house. Indeed, Wyatt had wanted an even more lavish effect, intending the walls to be yellow scagliola. The plasterwork *ceiling*, made in 1793 for £119, is one of Joseph Rose's best. The pilasters of mottled grey scagliola were made by Bartoli in 1794 to Wyatt's design. Rose supplied the Corinthian capitals the following year.

The semicircular *niches* with their exquisite little fan-vaults contain cast-iron *stoves* in the form of pedestals, which were later topped by Neo-classical urns. The mahogany *doors* were made by Hugh Finlay, John Berry and others. Inlaid with satinwood and decorated with panels possibly painted by Biagio Rebecca, they are remarkable demonstrations of 18th-century joinery, carefully curving to follow the oval form of the room.

Viscount Corry's 21st birthday party, September 1891

'The saloon was brilliantly lighted by many wax candles which saw themselves reflected in the long mirrors and polished floors over which… the dancers glided swiftly and easily.'

The Castle Coole Review

Furnishings

Not surprisingly, the 2nd Earl ordered especially lavish furniture and furnishings for what is the key social space in the house. For the *curtains*, he bought 'Striped Crimson Watered Satin', which was also used to upholster the furniture. They were lined with blue silk and elaborately decorated with gold silk fringing, silk tassels and ropes. The material has long since rotted away and had to be replaced, but the original gilt curtain poles, ornaments and pins still survive.

Preston also supplied almost all the furniture in this room, which comprises four gilt *lamp-stands*, the *mirrors* in gilt frames, the four gilt *couches* (which cost £272), the *sofa-tables*, two window *stools* and, in the centre of the room, the *circular table* with a rosewood and boullework top. The backs of the couches were curved to match the curve of the walls.

The very fine Broadwood *grand piano* has a case designed by Thomas Sheraton and is decorated with Wedgwood jasperware cameos and medallions. The 2nd Earl bought it in 1802 for his wife Juliana, who was a keen pianist. The cameos were later removed and used to decorate a Holland cabinet. David Hunt returned them when he restored the instrument in 1994.

(Right)
A cast-iron stove in the Saloon

(Far right)
The curved Saloon doors are decorated with panels which were possibly painted by Biagio Rebecca

15

The Drawing Room

This room concludes the sequence of state apartments on the ground floor and was originally the most formally set out in the house. By the late 19th century, it had become more informal and cluttered, with a piano and family photos on every surface. The family took afternoon tea here, when there were always generous quantities of sandwiches, scones and cake. They would re-gather here before supper and when it was announced, troop through the Saloon into the Dining Room. Afterwards, the ladies would return here to sit, read and talk before going to bed.

Decoration

Wyatt designed all the fixed decoration: ceiling plasterwork and anthemion and palmette frieze, doorcases and white marble chimneypiece. He intended the ceiling to be coloured pink and blue, but it was left off-white.

About 1816 blue wallpaper was put up to complement the Preston curtains and furnishings (see below). This was replaced by a white and gold leaf pattern in 1857, by which date the room had become a typically cluttered Victorian family sitting room. It was painted blue in the 1950s, but the result was not a success, and so it was repainted the present pale blue. The National Trust aims eventually to complete the restoration of Preston's grand scheme by reweaving his curtains.

The Aubusson *carpet* was introduced by the National Trust in 1952.

Curtains

The curtains supplied by Preston were the most magnificent in the house: 'Rich Striped Salmon

> 'The Drawing Room is to concentrate the elegance of the whole house.'
> Thomas Sheraton, *The Cabinet Dictionary*, 1803

Against the far wall is a French ebony and
ormolu (gilt bronze) *medal cabinet*. The large
pietra dura (hardstone) *table* was brought back
from Italy by the 2nd Earl.

Lighting

The chandelier was hung in 1986.

Pictures

From left to right on the far wall are portraits
of the builder of the house, the 1st Earl of
Belmore (painted by Robert Hunter), and his
first and third wives, Lady Margaret Butler (also
by Robert Hunter) and Mary Anne Caldwell
(by Hugh Douglas Hamilton). On the near
wall hang portraits of the 3rd Earl's wife,
Emily Louise Shepherd, and of the 4th Earl
(by Stephen Pearce).

Color Watered Satin', with a blue sarsenet
(fine silk) lining, salmon fringe and buff
and blue silk tassels. The fabric alone cost
over £1,000, and they came with richly
carved and gilded curtain poles. Despite
the protection of sun curtains, the curtain
silk had rotted away by the 1950s, when
they were taken down and replaced
with plainer Wyatt-style curtains.
(Wyatt had specified a striped red,
cream and blue pattern in 1791, but it
is doubtful whether his proposal was
ever implemented.) Currently, there are
muslin sun curtains.

Furniture

The 1st Earl left the room almost
unfurnished, apart from two pier-tables,
which have now gone. Preston supplied
the 2nd Earl with a suite of very grand
and expensive new gilt furniture, which
was upholstered with the same salmon-
coloured satin as the curtains. The
National Trust had the material rewoven
following unfaded fragments of the
original, which were found under a later
re-covering.

*(Right) Detail of a Preston sofa in the
Drawing Room*

17

The Stair Hall

The Stair Hall is effectively an extension of the Entrance Hall, and is treated in the same austere fashion, with the same Portland stone floor and no stair carpet or curtains.

Neo-classical architects like Wyatt enjoyed designing staircases that explored space and the limits of engineering. The upper flights of what is known as an 'imperial' staircase seem to float unsupported.

Decoration

What we see today was achieved only after much argument between the 1st Earl and Wyatt, whose initial scheme was rejected as too expensive. Belmore settled for a plain ceiling, but then opted for decorative plasterwork by Joseph Rose, which entailed adding a screen of Doric scagliola columns on the upper landing.

The iron *balustrade* is simple, but elegant, with gilded rosettes and a slim mahogany handrail.

Lighting

The room seems originally to have been lit only by the window over the half-landing, which allows light into the Entrance Hall through the fanlight over the door to the Hall. The present French ceiling *lantern* dates from about the 1860s.

Sculpture

On the half-landing is a bust by Turnerelli of the *Duke of Wellington*, who was by birth a member of the Anglo-Irish ascendancy. The 2nd Earl was a strong supporter and London neighbour of the Duke. The bust was here by 1903, when the

room was filled with swords, pistols and stirrups, and resembled 'a cross between a military museum, a gentleman's club, a post office and a day at the races'.

Pictures

The portraits are mainly of early 18th-century members of the Lowry-Corry family. They include Galbraith Lowry, whose marriage to Sarah Corry in 1733 united the Lowry and Corry families.

Furniture

The room contained no furniture until the late Victorian period. The rest of the set of Wyatt *hall-chairs* is now displayed here.

(Far right)
The plasterwork ceiling of the Stair Hall was made by Joseph Rose

(Right)
The Doric capital and cornice on the staircase

(Right) The Stair Hall

The Lobby

This grand, double-height space is the third in the sequence of rooms of passage, after the Entrance Hall and Stair Hall, and was designed and decorated to match. Because the Lobby occupies the centre of the house, it is lit by an oval skylight, which mirrors the oval form of the plasterwork on the Stair Hall ceiling, and two further circular skylights. At attic-floor level, a screen of enriched Doric columns painted to imitate marble runs round all four sides of the room, echoing the Stair Hall screen. The iron balustrade is also treated similarly.

The classically inspired stoves in the Lobby niches were probably designed by Wyatt

As in the Entrance Hall, there are semicircular niches, filled not with sculpture, but with classically inspired *stoves* (two real and two false), which are decorated with festoons, rams' heads and laurel wreaths. Installed in July 1796, they were probably designed by Wyatt and possibly supplied by the Dublin ironmonger George Binns or James Clark.

The *doors* on the long walls open directly into the two most important rooms on this

floor – the State Bedroom and the Bow Room. The other two doors lead to the principal bedrooms in the four corners.

The oak *floor* is especially fine.

Plasterwork

The plasterwork here is outstanding, both in quantity and quality, and is particularly easy to enjoy because this space is so well-lit and uncluttered. It features on the surround to the oval skylight, the doorcases, the dado rail and even the skirting boards.

Furniture

Wyatt intended the room to be unfurnished, but today it contains white-painted half-elliptical *side-tables* with slender French-style legs, designed by Wyatt.

The set of four ebonised *chairs* was supplied by Preston in 1809.

The State Bedroom

This is the most complete survivor of the Regency rooms that Preston created at Castle Coole. The State Bedroom was the traditional climax of the State Apartment – a sequence of rooms of increasing privacy and status found in baroque royal palaces such as Hampton Court. In baroque country houses, the state bedroom was set aside for the use of the monarch or other distinguished guests. By the early 19th century, such rooms had become very old-fashioned, but they remained an important status symbol.

The red flock *wallpaper* was made by J. & P. Boylan of Dublin in 1812.

State Bed

The bed is Preston's masterpiece. It is said to have been made for George IV's visit to Ireland in 1821, but in fact was commissioned several years before. It is a tester bed of Spanish mahogany, which is richly carved, especially on the bed-posts. The tester (canopy) is suspended from the ceiling and topped with an earl's coronet. The bed hangings are of scarlet silk with gilt fringes and ornaments, swagged like curtains. Some of the silk has had to be replaced, but the fringes and borders and the interior of the tester have survived intact. Flanking are the bed steps, which helped you to climb in.

Curtains

The original window curtains of 'Rich Fire Coloured Mantua [silk]' had disintegrated by the 1960s, when they were replaced, re-using the original trimmings. They were made to match the bed and came with three gilt curtain poles, which survive.

Other furniture

Preston also supplied a pair of marble-topped *commodes*, two large Grecian *armchairs*, eight (now six) mahogany *chairs* with caned seats made by W. Wray, and a mahogany *wardrobe*.

The black and gold lacquer *chest* at the foot of the bed is Chinese.

Pictures

These include engravings after William Hogarth's *Marriage à la Mode* series, one of his famous satires on mid-18th-century society. They are probably the set of Hogarth prints framed and glazed for Margetson Armar in 1748. Over the fireplace hangs *The Leslie Conversation-piece*.

The State Dressing Room

This room was decorated at the same time as the adjoining State Bedroom and to match. The curtains, draperies and wallpaper are all *en suite*. In the 1950s this was used by Wendy Lowry-Corry, one of Lord Belmore's sisters.

Furniture

The *bed* ('French Canopy Bed Stead') was supplied by Preston, although the hangings are simpler than he intended. He also provided the mahogany *dressing-table*. The *chairs* flanking the fireplace were used by the 7th Earl and Countess of Belmore at the Coronation in 1953.

Ceramics

The set of *bedroom china* bears the Belmore crest.

Pictures

On the far wall is a view of the eruption of Vesuvius in 1794, which was witnessed by the vulcanologist and British consul in Naples, Sir William Hamilton: 'Every operation of chymestry has been exhibiting, all sorts of airs produced, and the most curious electrical phenomena have been exhibited.'

(Left)
The State Bedroom

(Right)
The State Dressing Room

23

(Top) The Bow Room

(Above) The reprinted Chinoiserie curtains

*(Right) The Chinoiserie wallpaper in the Bow Room was
reprinted by the National Trust*

The Bow Room

The Bow Room lies immediately above the oval Saloon and shares its bow window, which enjoys fine views over Lough Coole. It was a private sitting room set aside for the ladies of the house, where they could write, read, play music or cards, and sew. In 1816 it was called the 'Work [i.e. needlework] Room', and the large window provided a steady north light ideal for this.

Decoration

This was one of the first rooms redecorated by Preston for the 2nd Earl. The grey and white Chinoiserie wallpaper was put up by Robert Dyas of Dublin in 1807, with 'Chinese chintz' (i.e. English glazed cotton) curtains and pelmets to match. These were all remade for the National Trust following pieces found behind a pier-glass in 1979–80, when Gervase Jackson-Stops and David Mlinaric re-presented the room on the basis of the 1816 inventory. They laid the rush-matting to suit the Chinoiserie mood of the room.

Furniture

Preston supplied the set of twelve satinwood *armchairs*, the pair of glass-fronted *cabinets*, and the *pier-tables* with gilt panther's-head legs of 1811. The frames of the *pier-glasses* also came from Preston, but the mirror-glass may be earlier.

The *sofas* are late 18th-century, and the bamboo *settee* and matching *chairs* were here by 1816. They are said to have come from Florence Court.

The *harp* was made by Sébastien and Pierre Erard, the *piano* by William Rolfe, *c.*1830.

Pictures

They include views of the Bay of Naples in the early 19th century and engravings after Claude-Joseph Vernet's *Ports of France*. Over the fireplace hangs a view of the Pont du Gard by Nathaniel Hone the Younger.

(Right) Gilt panther's-head leg on a pier-table

The Library

This was a comfortable family sitting room. In the early 20th century, the gentlemen would settle here to talk and smoke after supper.

Decoration

Wyatt made detailed designs for the ceiling, laurel wreath frieze, doorcases, bookcases, the picture hang and the fireplace. Only the last two were not executed. The present white marble *chimneypiece*, superbly carved to resemble drapery, was made by Westmacott in 1795 for £126 to a very different design. The walls were painted green in 1857.

Curtains

The curtains, which run along the entire window wall, were originally dark chocolate brown with a yellow lining, to match the sofas. The curtain-poles end in griffin heads, which feature on the Belmore crest and resemble a pattern found in George Smith's *A Collection of Designs* (1806). In 1857 the brown curtains were replaced with the present 'figured Crimson Silk Poplin' material, which is now very faded and worn.

Furniture

The large architectural *bookcases*, the semi-circular *pier-tables* and, probably, the *writing-desk* were all designed by Wyatt.

Preston supplied the two large Jamaican mahogany *sofas* (re-covered in the present deep red velvet by Gibson & Son of Dublin in 1857 to match the new curtains), two cane *armchairs* and the *overmantel mirror*, which all remain.

The terrestrial and celestial *globes* are typical library furniture.

Pictures

Between the windows are *The Falls of Marmora* and *Tivoli* by Antonio del Draco. Below them are Derek Hill's 1959 sketch of the Belmore Family, who are shown seated in the Saloon (the boy seated on the right is the present Lord Belmore), and David Jones's 1987 *Restoration of Castle Coole*. On the table are an oval pastel portrait of the *1st Earl* by Hugh Douglas Hamilton, and a pencil sketch of his second wife *Henrietta*, whom he divorced in 1793.

Books

This is a rare surviving example of an Irish Big House library. It still contains a significant number of books acquired by early generations of the Armar family. The 1st Earl bought many of the 18th-century works on agriculture. The library also reflects the 2nd Earl's passion for travel and his period as Governor of Jamaica (1828–32). The 4th Earl collected the very scarce examples of early Australian printing while Governor-General of New South Wales.

Viscount Corry's 21st birthday party, September 1891

'When wearied [the guests] rested in the library amid ferns and palms from the hot-houses, bull rushes and reed maces which the shores of the lake gave as their share in the festivities, while all around were gaily coloured silks etc brought from the East by the 2nd Earl of Belmore.'

The Castle Coole Review

(Right, top) The Library

(Right) Wyatt's design for the fireplace wall of the Library, showing the bookcases he designed and a suggested picture hang. The chimneypiece as carved by Richard Westmacott is very different

The Basement

Typically for a Neo-classical country house, the basement is sunk below ground level, but a broad light-well and tall sash-windows allow sunlight to penetrate it. A stone-vaulted tunnel four metres high and 50 metres long connects the east end of the house with the stables to the north-east, and was wide enough to allow carts to make deliveries to the Kitchen unseen. The bays were used for storing turf, wood and coal for the fires, and other bulky supplies.

The servants' quarters fill the entire basement and were planned on the grandest scale. The plasterwork and woodwork were plain, but of high quality, and, unlike the state rooms above, the basement was from the start comprehensively furnished throughout, with check curtains and mahogany furniture in the rooms used by the upper servants. Particularly impressive is the

high-vaulted Kitchen in the east wing, which remained in use until about 1950. Every other service function was given its own space, from a plunge bath to a room for powdering servants' wigs.

The National Trust is gradually opening these spaces for public access, restoring and conserving the fixtures and fittings.

The domestic offices in 1816

Kitchen	Butler's Pantry
Scullery	Butler's Bedroom
Scullery boys bedroom	Strong Closet [safe]
Larders	Men's Barrack Room
Bake House	Maid Servants' Bedrooms
Wine Cellars	Housekeeper's Room
Beer Cellar	Housekeeper's Bedroom
Servants Necessary [toilet]	[Wig] Powdering Room
Servants' Hall	Cook's Room
Bathing House	
Steward's Room	

Memories of Castle Coole in the early 20th century

'We were always taken down to the basement to see the Cook and I remember the large kitchen with its well-scrubbed wooden table and lots of polished copper cooking utensils hanging on the walls. The basement was an intriguing area for children.'

Brigadier G.W. Eden

Lighting the house

'Castle Coole was a nice place to work but they had no electricity. We had to use candles and oil lamps. The oddman and the butler used to light the lamps downstairs and along the passages. I looked after the ladies. There was a room for the 150 lamps which had to be cleaned and tended to daily. There were always two or three broken every morning so new glasses had to be got every month.'

Charles Battle, footman, 1929–36

The house staff in 1901

Name	Age	Occupation
Elfrida de Jaffa	26	Governess
Augusta Windruin	74	Housekeeper
Marion Forbes	38	Lady's maid
Susan Savil	20	Lady's maid
Mary Anne Crawford	25	Lady's maid
Mary Keenan	38	Cook
Sarah McCormick	32	Upper Housemaid
Catherine Houston	22	Housemaid
Jane Elliott	24	Housemaid
Annie Skeuse	19	Housemaid
Catherine Smyth	25	Housemaid
Mary Keir	18	Scullerymaid
Frederick Sudard	28	Butler
George Toombs	28	Footman

The Kitchen in 1936

The Park and Estate

John Corry bought the Manor Coole in 1655, and succeeding generations of his family added to the estate by purchase, inheritance and judicious marriage until it comprised, at its height, over 70,000 acres, spread across four counties: Longford, Monaghan, Tyrone and Fermanagh.

The early 18th-century formal garden

The first major development of the demesne (the Castle Coole estate) coincided with the building of the Queen Anne house in 1707. Col. James Corry's 1716 will noted 'great improvements in building and planting as well as of houses, gardens, orchards, as a large deer park, all walled and of great advantage as well as ornament'. The deer-park was created about 1707 a mile to the north of the house, and enclosed by a stone wall, most of which has now disappeared.

The next substantial changes were made in the mid-18th century by Margetson Armar. Between the house and lough, he laid out a formal garden which comprised raised parterres, a sunken bowling green, orchards and a water garden with a canal stretching 250 metres to the north-east. Raised platforms offered fine views over the whole scheme. A double oak avenue flanked the approach drives, and carriage drives were laid out through newly planted beech woods. The avenue remains the principal approach to the house to this day. Further afield, Armar improved roads and bridges, especially in Enniskillen, and acquired the nearby Churchlands estate.

A new demesne for a new house

In the early 1780s the 1st Earl began developing a new demesne at Castle Coole to improve the rental income of his estates and to complement his new house. In 1788–95 he created a new walled garden with heated greenhouses, which produced grapes, peaches, melons and cherries.

Artist's impression of Castle Coole in the mid-18th century, when the landscape was embellished with a canal and formal gardens

He drained boggy ground, enlarged fields, moved roads, added new gate lodges and planted huge numbers of trees in the naturalistic style that 'Capability' Brown had made fashionable on the other side of the Irish Sea. He commissioned an ice-house so that he

could preserve meats, and have cool drinks and ice-cream throughout the year. He also built a pump house to bring water from the lough up Fort Hill to the new house. The improvements were supervised by his clerk of works, Alexander Stewart, and his head gardener, William King, who had previously worked at Florence Court and Mount Stewart.

'To Eniskilling Lord Belmore's house at Castle Cool the most magnificent. The situation fine. The grounds exquisitely form'd. The trees finely scatter'd. Beautiful water. It wants, however, a apple [orchard?] and thick woods and great water to be answerable to the house.'

Thomas Russell's diary, 24 March 1793

The 19th century

Despite a shortage of money, in the early 19th century the 2nd Earl embarked on an ambitious revival of the estate woodlands, planting over 30,000 new trees. The new plantations were intended for pleasure as well as profit, providing the setting for hunting, shooting and fishing, to which the Earl was devoted. His wife Juliana focused on the kitchen garden, where new greenhouses were built to grow figs, grapes, pineapples and other tender soft fruit.

The Estate Yards

The stables attached to the Queen Anne house survived the latter's destruction by fire in 1797, and remained in use for some years. The 1st Earl had envisaged building new stables for his new house: indeed, the tunnel invisibly connecting them was dug at the same time as the foundations of the house. However, the work was not finally carried out until 1817, probably for lack of money. The 2nd Earl turned to the leading Irish architect Richard Morrison, who came up with an impressive and complex scheme to accommodate almost every conceivable requirement of the estate. The new yards were located 50 metres to the north-east of the house and hidden away from it by planting and the lie of the land. They comprised four main elements:

'Lakes are stocked with wild fowl, on one in particular, they are preserved with great care, the water seems almost covered with bold coots, wild ducks, widgeons, divers, teals, bitterns, wild geese and swans.'

Jonathan Binns, 1837

The Grand Yard

This handsome two-storey design was built of rendered rubble stone on the north side. The ground floor contained mainly stabling for the 2nd Earl's coaches and horses, especially his beloved hunters. Feed and stable staff were accommodated on the first floor. The inner courtyard was cobbled in decorative patterns, and sloped away from the pump at the centre to aid drainage.

The Laundry House

This comprised a wash-house, mangle, drying yard and even a 'smoothing room', where linen could be ironed. It also included a dairy yard and dairy kitchen. The tallow house (where candles would have been made) now serves as the visitor reception area. There were also two turf houses for storing turf for the fires. The Laundry has lost most of its interior fittings, and has been converted to private accommodation.

Richard Morrison's design for the Grand Yard

The Steward's House
(private: no public access)

Lying to the east, this elegant house with its unusual corner pilasters was built to house the 2nd Earl's steward, who managed his huge estate.

The Farm Yard
(private: no public access)

This contained the carpenter's and wheelwright's shops, together with the blacksmith's forge and shoeing shed, the slaughter house and stabling for the farm horses. There were also bullock, piggery and poultry yards, and a rick yard.

During the Second World War, these yards were taken over by the army. In the 1950s, parts of them were adapted for rearing chickens, but as they fell out of use, they became increasingly dilapidated. The National Trust acquired the Grand Yard and the Laundry Yard in the 1980s, and recognising the architectural and historical importance of these buildings, carried out essential repairs. Where interiors had been completely lost, they have been converted to accommodation to provide much-needed income. Lord Belmore still owns the Farm Yard and Steward's House, which are used as part of the working estate.

The last 150 years

The 4th Earl had even greater financial worries than his grandfather, but he continued to plant trees and in the 1850s created a new gate lodge and entrance drive between the house and the lough (the present visitor entrance). He also showed a paternalistic concern for the welfare of his tenants, for whom life became increasingly hard, particularly during 1846–7 – the desperate years of the Great Famine.

The 4th Earl was obliged to sell more and more of the outlying estates, but few major changes were made to the surviving core in the early 20th century. In 1957 commercial conifer

The Lowry-Corry sisters picking flowers in the Walled Garden

plantations were introduced to the south-east of the Grand Yard, and during the same decade 50 acres were leased to create the Enniskillen Golf Club.

In the care of the National Trust

The National Trust acquired 77 acres immediately surrounding the house in 1951, but in 1983, with the generous help of the National Heritage Memorial Fund, it was able to extend its protection to a further 315 acres, including the lough, the golf course and the principal parkland views from the house. The National Trust continues to manage the demesne in the traditional fashion, maintaining buildings, improving drainage, and planting and felling trees in order to preserve the historical integrity and visual beauty of the landscape, whilst at the same time allowing increasing public access to it. It also carries out regular biological surveys, which have revealed the unusual diversity of Castle Coole's flora and fauna.

The Lowry-Corrys of Castle Coole

Uniting three families

In 1641 John Corry, a Scottish merchant, settled in Belfast, where he prospered, investing the profits of his business in land. In 1655 he bought the Manor Coole in Co. Fermanagh, which included the 'castle' – a fortified settlement that had been built in 1611 by Captain Roger Atkinson as part of the early 17th-century Ulster Plantation. Corry died about 1683–5 and was succeeded by his son, Col. James Corry.

James Corry sided with his fellow Protestant William of Orange during the 'Glorious Revolution' of 1688, which ousted the Catholic King, James II. In his attempt to regain the throne, James raised an army in Ireland, which laid siege to the Protestant stronghold of Enniskillen. During the fighting, nearby Castle Coole was burnt to the ground to prevent it falling into enemy hands. Col. Corry subsequently claimed £1,000 in compensation for the loss of Castle Coole, but seems not to have rebuilt the house until 1707, when he was already in his late seventies. The new Castle Coole was a Dutch-style red-brick house of two main storeys with two parlours, a dining room and nine bedrooms, which was intended to accommodate his large extended family. It was sited near to the north-eastern shore of Lough Coole.

Col. Corry was succeeded in 1726 by his fourteen-year-old grandson Leslie Corry. During Leslie's minority, the estate was managed by his cousin, Margetson Armar, who had been brought up at Castle Coole and who married Leslie's sister Mary in 1736. Armar was effectively master of Castle Coole between 1726 and 1773, because, when Leslie Corry died young, unmarried and without an adult male Corry heir in 1741, he handed over responsibility for the running of the estate to his trusted brother-in-law. Armar devoted his life to improving the Castle Coole demesne, laying new drains and planting broad shelter belts of trees. His wife Mary was a talented gardener, who laid out a formal garden between the house and the lough and constructed heated greenhouses in the kitchen garden.

By the 1740s, Col. Corry's house must have seemed somewhat old-fashioned. In 1747 Armar began a campaign of thorough-going modernisation. His account book reveals that he installed new carved marble chimneypieces and laid Scotch (woven wool) carpets. Large sums were spent on flock wallpaper and damask curtains. He also commissioned a portrait of his wife from

(Far left)
Col. James Corry
(c.1633–1718)

(Left)
Col. John Corry
(1666–1726)

(Right)
Margetson Armar
(1700–73), who married
John Corry's daughter
Mary and ran the estate
during the mid-18th
century

(Right)
Leslie Corry (1712–41)

(Far right)
Galbraith Lowry (1706–69), who took the name Corry after marrying John Corry's daughter Sarah in 1733. Their son built the present house

Francis Bindon (who was a better architect than a painter) and paid for framing and glazing a set of Hogarth engravings. Both the portrait and the prints are still at Castle Coole.

Margetson and Mary Armar had no children, and all these improvements were being carried out on behalf of their young nephew, on whom their dynastic hopes rested. Both in his name and in his person, Armar Lowry-Corry was to unite three families and to create Castle Coole as we know it today. Born in 1740, he was the son of Mary's sister Sarah and of Galbraith Lowry,

the MP for Tyrone, who changed his name to Lowry-Corry in 1764 as a condition of their son inheriting the Corry estates. Armar Lowry-Corry finally inherited the Armar, Lowry and Corry estates in 1779, after the deaths in rapid succession of Margetson Armar, Mary Armar and Sarah Lowry-Corry.

Castle Coole could now be transformed.

(Below) John Curle's design for the Queen Anne house, which was destroyed by fire in 1797

Armar, 1st Earl of Belmore (1740–1802), who built the new house

Armar Lowry-Corry, 1st Earl of Belmore (1740–1802)

Armar Lowry-Corry was his parents' much-loved third, but only surviving, son. He was educated at home and trained by his father in estate management. He grew up to love the outdoor life of hunting, shooting and fishing, which the Castle Coole demesne was well equipped to satisfy. In 18th-century Ireland, just as in England, land equalled power – represented here politically by the Irish parliament in Dublin. Armar succeeded his father as MP for Tyrone in 1769, and adopted the independent line of a wealthy country gentleman. In 1771 he married the 1st Earl of Carrick's daughter, Lady Margaret Butler, who produced a son and heir, but died young in 1776. On his mother's death in 1779 Armar Lowry-Corry came into the Corry estates, which, with his other inheritances, comprised over 70,000 acres and generated an annual income of £11,000.

Lowry-Corry's second wife was Lady Henrietta Hobart, the daughter of the Earl of Buckinghamshire, who was Lord Lieutenant of Ireland at the time. It was another dynastic

Mary Anne Caldwell (d.1841), the 1st Earl's third wife

alliance (Lowry-Corry was created Lord Belmore as part of the deal) rather than a love match. Henrietta was 22 years younger than Belmore and was not consulted during the marriage negotiations. Perhaps unsurprisingly, therefore, she disliked the remote old house at Castle Coole, and she disliked Belmore. What was more, she made no attempt to hide her dislike. In 1781, after only a year of marriage, Belmore demanded a separation, which Henrietta was delighted to accept. She left Ireland and subsequently fell in love with and married Lord Ancram, after a divorce was eventually agreed in 1793. Lord Belmore's personal unhappiness seems not to have held back his ambitious plans to transform the Castle Coole demesne with a grand new house, which was rising fast from the early 1790s (see p. 38).

Belmore's third marriage, to Mary Anne Caldwell in 1794, was much more tranquil, but almost ended in tragedy. At the age of 43, Mary Anne became pregnant and came very close to dying in childbirth. She survived, but preferred to convalesce in Bath, where Belmore spent many of his declining years and died in 1802.

(Left) Lady Margaret Butler (d.1776), the 1st Earl's first wife

(Above, top) Wyatt's design for the entrance front

(Above) Wyatt's design for the garden front

Building the house

The Queen Anne house built by his grandfather was hardly adequate for a man of Lord Belmore's wealth, social status and political ambition. He seems to have been spurred on to build by his intense rivalry with the Marquess of Abercorn, with whom he battled for political supremacy in Co. Tyrone. Belmore also wanted to go one better than his brother-in-law, Lord Enniskillen, who had rebuilt nearby Florence Court 20 years before.

Belmore suffered from rheumatism (his library contained medical treatises on the affliction). So when he decided to build a new house on the Coole demesne in 1788, he settled on an airy site on Forth Hill up the slope from the lough and the damp old house. Creating a level terrace for the new house involved digging twelve feet into the hillside. Richard Johnston, a Dublin architect, produced the earliest surviving designs, which are dated 14 October 1789, and the foundations were dug following these

proposals, with the entrance front facing up the slope and away from the lough. However, Belmore was an exacting client, and he seems to have lost faith in Johnston. Between October 1789 and May 1790 he called in James Wyatt, perhaps at the suggestion of his father-in-law, Lord Buckinghamshire, with whom he remained on good terms despite the divorce, and who had employed Wyatt's brother Samuel at Blickling Hall in Norfolk.

James Wyatt was one of the most skilful and fashionable exponents of the Neo-classical style. He was also frantically busy, and although he had a substantial Irish practice, he never visited Castle Coole. The design he conceived for Lord Belmore was altogether more sophisticated than Johnston's initial scheme. Working within the footprint of the foundations that had already been dug, Wyatt increased the scale of the flanking wings, and pared down external detail to the absolute minimum: the windows became plain openings without any form of decorative surround, and the urns suggested by Johnston were banished from the rooftop balustrade. The grandeur of the new house depended chiefly on its perfectly judged proportions and the superb quality of the materials used.

The bricks and ironwork for the new house were made on site, but the facing stone which is the splendour of Castle Coole was imported all the way from the Portland quarries in Dorset in Lord Belmore's brig *Martha*. He had a quay specially built at Ballyshannon, where the stone was transferred to barges which carried it up Lough Erne to Enniskillen. The final stage of its long journey to Castle Coole was made by cart. Construction was supervised by Belmore's Scottish clerk of works, Alexander Stewart, who had earlier worked on Baronscourt, the Tyrone home of Belmore's great rival, Lord Abercorn. The master mason was William Cane. The west wing was roofed in 1791, the central block in 1792, and the east wing in 1793; the great Ionic portico was up by 1794.

Castle Coole's plan is more English than Irish. Distinguished visitors would be greeted in the Hall at the centre of the entrance front, and then – depending on their status – be ushered into the flanking Library or the Breakfast Room. The central block, with its grand Saloon, was set aside for the kind of formal entertaining that was intended to promote Belmore's political ambitions. Family life was carried on in the more modest wings, which had their own everyday entrances. Servants were segregated in their vast basement quarters and rendered invisible by separate staircases and the broad tunnel that linked the basement to the Grand Yard.

Wyatt provided detailed designs for ceiling plasterwork and friezes, chimneypieces, doorcases, bookcases and furniture, all in an appropriately spare Neo-classical style. The best craftsmen were employed, including the sculptor Richard Westmacott for the marble chimneypieces; the scagliola specialist Domenico Bartoli; and the plasterer Joseph Rose, who became increasingly exasperated at Belmore's frequent changes of mind.

Much of what Wyatt had intended was not carried out, often for reasons of cost. Belmore had planned to build the house out of income, but this proved wildly unrealistic. By July 1795 he had already spent over £50,000 (the final bill came to £70,000), and even a man of his substantial resources was forced to cut back. The house was still not ready for occupation the following summer, when De la Tocnaye made his visit in 1796, which may explain his comment that 'comfort has been almost entirely sacrificed to beauty'. However, Belmore had no choice but to move in when the old house burnt down in the summer of 1797 after a spark from a pan of hot ashes ignited the staircase. Family portraits and furniture were rescued from the flames, but the new house (the interior of which was painted off-white throughout) must still have been very sparsely furnished.

The completion of the house in 1797 coincided with Belmore receiving an earldom, but he had difficulty savouring either achievement. By this stage he was in failing health, and all his hopes for Castle Coole and the family were focused on his son and heir, Somerset, Viscount Corry.

The Saloon is the climax of Wyatt's suite of state rooms

'Boundless expense'
Somerset, 2nd Earl of Belmore (1774–1841)

At the age of about sixteen, Somerset Lowry-Corry injured his right leg, which left him lame for the rest of his life. But this never seems to have stopped him hunting on the Castle Coole estate or indulging his passion for travel. He also bred and raced horses at the Curragh. When he came of age in 1795, his income and responsibilities expanded, and he became increasingly involved in fighting his ailing and absent father's political battles. He campaigned fiercely against the Act of Union, which sought to abolish the independent Irish parliament in Dublin, but was ultimately defeated in 1800. When he succeeded his father as 2nd Earl in 1802, he inherited huge debts incurred by their political campaigning and by building the new house, but this does not seem to have stopped him spending still more.

The 2nd Earl had three main objectives in life: to rebuild his political career after defeat on the Union; to complete Castle Coole; and to travel.

> 'Lord Belmore is a rich extravagant young man, he won't deign to keep a House in Dublin, has a magnificent one in the Country, that he is going to furnish with boundless expense.'
>
> Andrew Caldwell, January 1806

Seeking power

Now that the centre of power had moved from Dublin to London, he sold his house in the Irish capital, together with all its furniture, much of which was brand new and had never been unpacked. He re-established his political base in London, where he bought a house, but it was not until 1819 that he achieved his aim of acquiring an English 'representative' peerage, which would allow him to sit in the House of Lords in Westminster.

Furnishing the house

When the 2nd Earl inherited Castle Coole, it still had little furniture, and Wyatt's spartan style of Neo-classical decoration was going out of fashion. Regency luxury was now the thing. So in 1807 he commissioned the Dublin cabinet-makers and dealers John and Nathaniel Preston to furnish the principal rooms with massive gilt and mahogany pieces in a lavish French Empire style; most are still in the house. The Prestons' total bill came to a staggering £26,367, but the 2nd Earl was still spending in 1810, when he bought yet more furniture at the Earl of Clonmell's sale in Dublin. In the same year, work began on a new service block, which included stables, designed by Sir Richard Morrison and known as the Grand Yard.

(Left) The richly gilded sofas in the Saloon were supplied by the Dublin upholsterer John Preston

(Right) Somerset, 2nd Earl of Belmore (1774–1841), who furnished his father's house in lavish style

The Osprey, *in which the 2nd Earl and his family cruised the Mediterranean*

Travels

As a young man, the 2nd Earl had made a voyage around the Mediterranean, which seems to have inspired his love of travel. It was also a way of dispelling boredom and escaping his creditors. In 1813 he bought an American schooner, which he renamed the *Osprey* and fitted out at considerable expense with new furniture and WCs. Taking his whole family, a large household staff and a crew of 30, in August 1816 he set off on a four-year voyage to explore Egypt and the Holy Land. By September 1817 the party had reached Cairo, from where they set off to view the pyramids at Giza. Encouraged by the archaeologist Henry Salt, he decided to make a pioneering journey up the Nile. The 2nd Earl was so impressed by the temple of Dendara at Thebes that he sponsored excavation of the site and began a collection of Egyptian antiquities, which was 'the largest ever made

by any occasional traveller', according to a contemporary witness. He was also one of the first Europeans to see the recently excavated tomb of the pharaoh Rameses I in the Valley of the Kings. After reaching as far as the second cataract on the Nile, they returned to Cairo, where they packed up their accumulated treasures, which the 2nd Earl sold to the British Museum in 1842 to pay off debts. They travelled overland to Syria and Palestine, and returned home via Italy, acquiring on the way more conventional Grand Tour trophies, including Etruscan vases, Roman armour, marble tables and bronzes (most notably, Giuseppe Piamontini's superb equestrian statue of Ferdinando de' Medici).

Belmore was welcomed back at Castle Coole by his tenants in the spring of 1820, but having spent £4,000 on the voyage, he also faced increasingly severe money problems. Even so, he still felt able to commission a grandiose and expensive state bed from the Prestons. In 1823 he held an extravagant party to celebrate the coming-of-age of his eldest son.

Jamaica

Having failed to achieve political preferment at home, the 2nd Earl looked abroad. In 1828 he was appointed Governor of Jamaica with the support of his friend, the Duke of Wellington, who was prime minister at the time. He arrived to find the island in turmoil. The local assembly, which was dominated by white plantation owners, resented interference by the British government, which wanted to improve the miserable conditions of the 300,000 black slaves on the island. The 2nd Earl's awkward position between these two warring parties was made worse by the appointment of Lord Goderich as Colonial Secretary in 1830. In December 1831 slaves on the west of the island rebelled – the most serious revolt in Jamaican history. Martial law was declared, and the army and militia restored order after summarily executing the ring leaders. The British government needed a scapegoat and found one in Lord Belmore, who was recalled in disgrace, but whose conduct was subsequently vindicated.

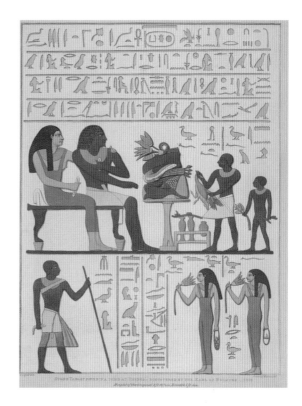

(Above, right)
Stone tablet found in a tomb at Thebes by the 2nd Earl in 1818. Illustrated in Lord Belmore's Collection of Egyptian Antiquities *(1822)*

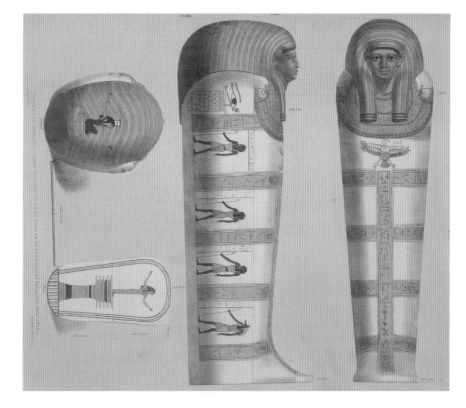

(Right)
Stone sarcophagus taken out of a tomb at Thebes by the 2nd Earl in 1818. Illustrated in Lord Belmore's Collection of Egyptian Antiquities *(1822)*

The 19th century

Armar, 3rd Earl of Belmore (1801–45)

The 2nd Earl's son, Armar, expressed his
devotion to Castle Coole in childhood verse:

Soon to my native house I will repair
And to those things which give me pleasure there,
My little island, ever neat and gay;
The parrot's talk or puppies lively play…
Dear abode of happiness! My home!
O Castle Coole to thee I long to come.

But he was to own the estate for only four years,
dying in 1845 at the age of 44.

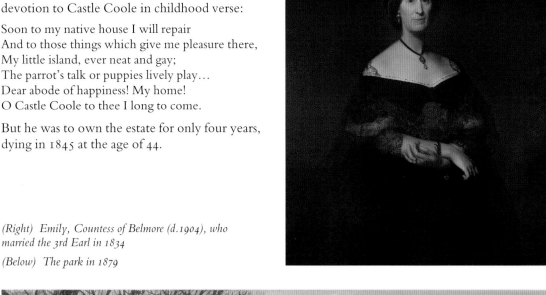

*(Right) Emily, Countess of Belmore (d.1904), who
married the 3rd Earl in 1834*

(Below) The park in 1879

Somerset, 4th Earl of Belmore (1835–1913)

The 4th Earl's reign at Castle Coole was to be altogether longer, reaching almost to the First World War. But the estate he inherited at the age of nine was in a parlous financial state. To avoid bankruptcy, he had to place it under the protection of the Chancery Court. With the understanding support of his mother and grandmother, he managed to rescue his position, but he was forced to sell outlying properties in the 1850s. The core of the Castle Coole estate was 'reduced to a mere 20,000 acres', as he put it. In 1857 he managed to find the money to redecorate the house and lay out a new drive with a new gate lodge.

The 4th Earl inherited the family fascination with politics. In 1861 he married Anne Honoria Gladstone, the niece of the future prime minister. (On the other side of the political divide, his cousin Montagu Corry was Disraeli's devoted private secretary.) Much of the 4th Earl's time was spent away from Ireland engaged in behind-the-scenes committee work at Westminster. He became particularly expert in the minutiae of railway finance, but he needed a job that paid a salary. So in 1867 he accepted the Governor-Generalship of New South Wales. During his tenure, an attempt was made to assassinate Queen Victoria's son, the Duke of Edinburgh. The Duke's attacker, Henry James O'Farrell, was thought to be a Fenian terrorist, but there was no evidence, and Belmore skilfully succeeded in defusing a potentially dangerous political situation. The 4th Earl toured the country extensively and supported the development of railways throughout Australia.

In 1871 the 4th Earl returned home because his wife Honoria was in poor health, but she still managed to bear him thirteen children who survived infancy. The east wing was turned into a nursery with a schoolroom that was filled with toys and improving religious tracts. Castle Coole became a typically cluttered Victorian home. The children rode on the estate, worked in the kitchen garden, performed amateur dramatics and contributed to the house newspaper, the *Castle Coole Review*. In the summer there were cricket matches on a pitch laid out on the site of the former formal garden of the old house. Life carried on at Castle Coole with little apparent change for the rest of the 4th Earl's long life, despite the worsening financial position for Irish landlords. The 4th Earl was an invalid in his later years, when he withdrew to the west wing to devote himself to his scholarly researches. He wrote two learned family histories, which remain important sources.

(Right) Somerset, 4th Earl of Belmore (1835–1913)

Modern times

The 5th Earl of Belmore (1870–1948) never married, but the house was rarely empty during the inter-war years, as five unmarried siblings lived on in the house together. But because the house was 'dry', they were not often troubled by visiting relations. The 5th Earl was succeeded in 1948 by his younger brother Cecil, who was also unmarried and lived on for only one more year. At this point, the title passed to a great-nephew of the 4th Earl, Major Galbraith Lowry-Corry, who moved into Castle Coole, but could no longer afford the growing costs of running it. In 1951 the house and 70 acres were acquired by the National Trust thanks to a grant from the Ulster Land Fund. The present 8th Earl, who was born in 1951, continues to live on the estate with his family and maintains a close interest in all that happens here.

Restoring Castle Coole

Castle Coole was not built from solid stone, but with a thin skin of squared-off blocks, which were attached at each corner with iron cramps to the load-bearing wall of rubble stone behind. Over the decades, water had penetrated the joints between the blocks and rusted the cramps, causing them to expand and crack the corners of the blocks. The smooth perfection of Castle Coole's Portland stone façades was becoming increasingly pockmarked.

In 1980 the National Trust decided that repair was essential. Rather than making piecemeal replacements with new stone (the traditional Arts and Crafts solution), the Trust took down the entire external cladding. It replaced the rusted cramps with stainless steel, reused the original blocks wherever possible, and replaced the rest with new stone from the same Portland

A stone mason removing the damaged Portland stone cladding the house

The east wing after conservation of the stonework

quarry. The work was carried out by a team of twelve under master mason Eddie McKibbin. As often happens, removing the broken stonework revealed further problems such as rotting roof trusses, which had to be put right. The project took seven years and cost £3.2 million, which was funded by the Northern Ireland Department of the Environment, National Heritage Memorial Fund and the National Trust. Castle Coole regained its crisp perfection, and almost 30 years later, it is difficult to distinguish old stone from new. The National Trust also took the opportunity to redecorate the principal rooms, following extensive research and analysis of the documentary and physical evidence.

Looking to the future

Castle Coole's small, but dedicated staff continues to work with limited resources to make the whole property more accessible to visitors. Already, over 250,000 people use the park every year to find physical and spiritual refreshment in an increasingly urbanised landscape, but the National Trust is keen to involve them more directly in its continuing conservation work. It is gradually opening up the huge servants' quarters in the basement, drawing on the memories of many local people who worked here in order to interpret these atmospheric spaces. The Trust also plans to conserve the fraying Library curtains and remake the equally magnificent Preston curtains in the Drawing Room, so that Castle Coole will remain for years to come the grand 'palace in the park' it has always been.

The Lowry-Corry Family of Castle Coole

James Lowry (d. 1665)
settled at Ballimagory, Co. Tyrone before 1641

JOHN CORRY (d. 1683–5) = Blanch Johnston
bought Castle Coole 1656

John Lowry = (1) Mary Buchanan
(d. 1689) of Aghenis, (2) Jane Hamilton
Co. Tyrone

Col. JAMES CORRY* = (1) Sarah Ankerell, m. 1663
(c.1633–1718) (2) Lucy Mervyn, m. 1683
(3) Elizabeth Harryman, m. 1691

Robert Lowry = Anna Sinclair
(d. 1729) of Aghenis

Col. JOHN CORRY* = Sarah Leslie
(1666–1726) m.1701

Galbraith = SARAH*
Lowry-Corry* (1709–79)
(1706–69) m. 1733
assumed name and arms
of Corry 1764

Martha*
(1704–64)
= Capt Edmund
Leslie
m. 1738

MARY*
(1710–74)
= Col. MARGETSON
ARMAR*
(1700–73)

Leslie*
(1712–41)

Elizabeth* (1715–91)
= (1) Archibald Hamilton
m. 1751–2
(2) James Leslie,
m. 1754

ARMAR LOWRY-CORRY* = (1) Margaret* (d. 1776) dau. of 1st Earl of Carrick
(1740–1802) m. 1771
cr. Baron 1781, Viscount 1789, (2) Henrietta* (1762–1805) dau. of 2nd Earl of
1st EARL OF BELMORE 1797 Buckinghamshire m. 1780, div. 1793
built present Castle Coole (3) Mary Anne Caldwell* (d. 1841) m. 1794

Anna = William, 1st Earl
(1743–1803) of Enniskillen
(1736–1803)
m. 1763

SOMERSET, 2nd EARL OF BELMORE* = Juliana, dau. of 2nd Earl of Carrick
(1774–1841) (d. 1861) m.1800

ARMAR, 3rd EARL OF BELMORE = Emily Louise Shepherd*
(1801–45) (1814–1904) m. 1834

SOMERSET, 4th EARL OF BELMORE* = Anne Honoria Gladstone*
(1835–1913) (d. 1919) m. 1861

Admiral the Hon. Armar = Geraldine King King
Lowry-Corry (1836–1919) (d.1905) m. 1868

ARMAR, 5th EARL OF BELMORE
(1870–1948)

CECIL, 6th EARL OF BELMORE
(1873–1949)

Adrian Lowry-Corry = Geraldine Hartcup
(1876–1921) (d. 1944) m. 1909

(1) GALBRAITH ARMAR, 7th EARL OF BELMORE* = Gloria Harker* = (2) Col. Robert Irwin MC
(1913–60) m. 1939 (d. 2005) (d. 1984)

Lady Anthea* = Patrick Forde
(b. 1942) (d. 2008)
m. 1965

Lady Sarah* = G. McNulty
(b. 1945) m. 1979

JOHN ARMAR, = Mary Jane, dau. of
8th EARL OF BELMORE* 6th Earl of Clanwilliam
(b. 1951) m. 1984

Heads of the family resident at Castle Coole
are indicated in CAPITALS

* Asterisk denotes portrait at Castle Coole

John Armar Galbraith,
Viscount Corry
(b. 1985)

Montagu
Gilford George
(b. 1989)

Martha
Catherine
(b. 1992)